Logic for

Children

Concepts and Exercises

Decio Martins de Medeiros

This book was created with the assistance of artificial intelligence, using ChatGPT for generating texts and illustrations.

Bibliographic Information:
Author: Decio Martins de Medeiros.
Title: Logic for Children.
Subtitle: Concepts and Exercises.
Location, Year: São Paulo-Brazil, 2024.
Pages: 71 pages, 6"x9" size.
Subjects: 1. Logic

Table of Contents

0-Teaching Children to Think

Edward De Bono argued that, instead of just learning facts and procedures, children should be taught to think critically, creatively, and constructively.

De Bono also criticized the traditional approach to education, which often emphasizes memorization and linear thinking, at the expense of stimulating the ability to solve problems creatively. He believed that if children were taught to develop these skills from an early age, they could grow up to be more innovative, adaptable, and successful adults.

He developed practical methods for this, such as the Six Thinking Hats, a tool used to encourage thinking from different perspectives, and believed that this type of approach could transform the way students tackle problems, not only in school but also in everyday life.

A book that teaches logical thinking to children should have a clear and gradual progression, respecting the children's cognitive development level. Start with concrete concepts and gradually move towards more complex abstractions, always with practical examples and fun activities.

1-Introduction to Logical Thinking

Hi, everyone! Today we're going to talk about something really cool and super useful: logical thinking! But what does that mean, and why is it so important? Let's find out together!

What is logical thinking?

Logical thinking is about using your brain to solve problems in an organized, step-by-step way. Imagine you have a puzzle to complete: you need to look at the pieces, think about how they fit together, and connect them until you form the picture. That's logical thinking in action!

We use logical thinking in many parts of our day:

- **At school**, when solving math problems or answering questions in class.
- **In games**, like when playing chess or video games and planning your next moves.
- **At home**, when figuring out the best way to do tasks, like tidying your room or helping in the kitchen.

Where do we use logical thinking?

Logical thinking shows up in many moments of the day, often without us even noticing. It's there when:

- **Making important decisions**, like deciding what to do first on your homework.
- **Solving problems**, like figuring out why your bike isn't working properly.
- **Understanding the world around us**, like noticing that when you throw a ball up, it comes back down.

Why is logical thinking important?

Now that we know what it is, let's see why logical thinking is so important! It helps us in many ways:

1. **Problem-solving:** Logical thinking allows us to stay calm and find solutions to everyday challenges. If something isn't working, logic helps you figure out what to do to fix it.
2. **Making better decisions:** Sometimes we need to choose what to do first or how to act in a situation. Logical thinking helps us see the best choice and understand why.
3. **Organizing ideas and tasks:** Using logic makes it easier to organize things. It helps plan the day, complete tasks in order, and even understand school lessons better.
4. **Understanding how things work:** The world around us follows rules, and logical thinking helps us understand them. For example, you know that mixing water and soap creates bubbles, right? That's logic!

How to improve logical thinking?

You can train your logical thinking in fun ways, such as:

- **Puzzle games:** Sudoku, chess, or building with Lego can help develop logic.
- **Solving problems:** Think about daily situations like, "If I have 10 candies and eat 2, how many are left?" That's logic!
- **Observing patterns:** Try finding patterns around you. For example, if numbers follow a sequence like "2, 4, 6, 8...," what's next? Spotting patterns is great for improving logical thinking.

Logical thinking is a superpower!

Now that you know what logical thinking is and why it's important, you can use it in any situation. Solving problems, making good decisions, and organizing ideas will become much easier. Logical thinking is like a superpower you can always rely on!

So, the next time you face a challenge, remember to use your logical superpower to overcome it!

2-Basic Concepts of Logic

Hi, everyone! Today we're going to learn about logic, which is a way of using your brain to think and solve problems. We'll talk about two very important concepts: facts and assumptions, and the difference between true and false. Ready to get started?

What Are Facts?

A fact is something that is real and true, something that actually happened or exists. For example:

- The sun rises every morning.
- Water is wet.
- 2 + 2 = 4.

These things are facts because we can prove they're true. Everyone can see and test them, and they don't change no matter what happens.

What Are Assumptions?

An assumption is something we think or imagine, but we're not sure if it's true. It's like an idea that still needs to be proven. For example:

- I think it's going to rain today.
- My friend might be at home right now.
- Maybe I'll get a good grade on the test.

These are assumptions because we don't know for sure. You can make assumptions all the time, but they're not always right.

Difference Between True and False

Now that we know what facts and assumptions are, let's understand the difference between true and false.

- Something true is what really happens, what is a fact. For example, "The Earth revolves around the sun" is true because it's a fact we can prove.
- Something false is what isn't real, what doesn't actually happen. For example, "The moon is made of cheese" is false because we know the moon isn't made of cheese, right?

How to Tell What's True or False

To find out if something is true or false, you can ask questions and look for proof! Here are some examples:

- If someone says 2 + 2 = 5, you can check by doing the math and see that it's false. The truth is 2 + 2 = 4!
- If someone says it will rain tomorrow, you can't be sure because it's an assumption. Only when tomorrow comes will you know if it's true or false.

Using Logic to Think Better

When you start using logic, you can separate things that are facts from those that are just assumptions, and that helps you figure out what's true or false. This makes it easier to make smarter decisions and understand what's going on around you.

Let's practice a bit! If someone says, "Fish live in water," is that a fact or an assumption? That's right, it's a fact because we know fish live in water. But if someone says, "I think there will be cake at the party," that's an assumption because they're not sure, right?

Conclusion

Now you know what facts, assumptions, and the differences between true and false are. Using logic is a smart way to think and solve problems, and it will help you make better decisions every day!

So whenever you're in doubt, remember to use your head and think carefully: Is this a fact or an assumption? Is it true or false? You'll become a true detective of logic!

3-Sequences and Patterns

Hello, everyone! Today, we're going to talk about something really cool that can be found in many places: sequences and patterns! We'll learn what they are, how to identify them, and even how to create our own patterns. Ready? Let's get started!

What are patterns?

A pattern is something that repeats in an organized way. It could be a sequence of colors, shapes, numbers, or anything that follows a specific order. For example, if you look at a brick wall, you'll notice that the bricks are arranged in a repeating way. That's a pattern!

Some examples of patterns are:

- **Repeated colors**: red, blue, red, blue, red... What's the next color? Blue, right? Because the pattern is red and blue repeating.
- **Shapes**: circle, square, circle, square... What comes next? A circle!

How to identify patterns?

Identifying patterns is like solving a mystery. You need to observe carefully and figure out what is repeating. Let's look at an example:

Imagine you see the following sequence of numbers: 2, 4, 6, 8... Can you spot the pattern? Yes! The pattern is adding 2 to each number. If the pattern continues, what will the next number be? It'll be 10!

So, identifying patterns is about finding the "rule" that makes something repeat.

Creating your own patterns

Now that we know how to identify patterns, how about creating our own? You can create patterns in many ways:

- **Colors**: Choose some colors and make a repeating sequence, like: yellow, green, green, yellow, green, green...
- **Shapes**: Create a sequence of shapes, like: triangle, circle, circle, triangle, circle, circle...
- **Numbers**: Try creating a number pattern. For example, choose to add 3 to each number: 3, 6, 9, 12...

When you create your own patterns, you can make as many combinations as you want! Use your imagination!

Completing sequences

Besides identifying and creating patterns, we can also complete sequences that have already started. Let's practice with some examples:

Numerical sequences

Look at this sequence: 5, 10, 15, 20... What's the next number? If you noticed we're adding 5, the next number will be 25!

Visual sequences

Now, look at this sequence of shapes: circle, square, circle, square... What comes next? A circle! That's a visual pattern.

Logical sequences

Now think of a logical sequence. For example: "In the morning, the sun rises, in the afternoon it's high in the sky, and at night it sets." What happens after night? The sun rises again in the morning! That's an example of a logical pattern, something that happens repeatedly every day.

Why are sequences and patterns important?

Identifying and creating patterns is very important because it helps your brain think in an organized way. When you recognize patterns, you can solve problems faster and understand how things work better.

Also, patterns are everywhere:

- **In nature**: the cycle of the seasons follows a pattern.
- **In math**: multiplication tables are full of patterns!
- **In music**: notes follow a sequence to create a melody.

Conclusion

Now that you know what sequences and patterns are, how about trying to create your own? Remember that patterns can be found in numbers, colors, shapes, and even in nature. The more you train your eye to notice these repetitions, the better you'll get at solving problems and understanding the world around you!

So, have fun identifying and creating your own patterns. Who knows—you might discover an amazing new pattern!

4-Classification and Grouping

Hello, everyone! Today we're going to learn about classifying and grouping objects. This means organizing things in a way that makes sense, using characteristics like color, shape, or size. Let's find out how it works!

What does it mean to classify?

Classifying means sorting objects into groups based on their characteristics. Characteristics are things we can see or feel, like color, size, or shape. For example:

- If you have a bunch of colored pencils, you can classify them by color: put the red ones together, the blue ones together, the yellow ones together, and so on.
- If you have several toys, you can classify them by size: big toys on one side and small toys on the other.

Classifying helps us put things in order and makes it easier to find what we need!

Grouping objects by characteristics

When you group objects, you put together those that have something in common. Let's look at some examples of how we can group:

- **By color:** Imagine you have several balls of different colors. You can make a group of red balls, a group of green balls, a group of blue balls, and so on.
- **By shape:** If you have toys with various shapes, you can put all the round toys in one group, square toys in another, and triangular toys in another.
- **By size:** If you have big and small dolls, you can make one group for big dolls and another for small dolls.

Organizing objects

Now that we know how to classify and group, let's talk about organizing. Organizing means arranging things neatly and making them easy to find. Imagine how messy it would be if all your toys were mixed up! Organizing is a way to keep everything in the right place.

For example, if you were organizing your clothes, you could put:

- T-shirts in one drawer,
- Pants in another,
- Socks in another.

That way, when you're picking out what to wear, it's much easier because everything is in the right spot!

Let's practice!

Now it's your turn! Look around you and see if you can find things to classify and group. Here are some ideas:

- Classify your colored pencils into groups by color.
- Separate bigger toys from smaller toys.
- Organize your Lego pieces by shape or size.

When you do this, you'll notice how much easier it is to find things and keep your space tidy.

Why is classifying and grouping important?

Classifying and grouping objects is a very important skill because we use it all the time, even without realizing it. When you help tidy up the house or organize your school supplies, you're using these skills! Plus, classifying and grouping help your brain become smarter and quicker at solving problems.

Conclusion

Now you know how to classify and group objects using characteristics like color, shape, and size. Classifying and organizing the things around you makes everything easier and more fun. So, how about practicing and organizing your things today? I bet it'll be fun!

5-Comparison and Contrast

Hi, everyone! Today, we're going to talk about how to compare things and find what they have in common or what makes them different. This is called comparison and contrast. Let's see how it works and how it can help us solve problems.

What does it mean to compare?

To compare is to look at two or more things and see what they have in common. For example, think about an apple and an orange. They're different, but they also have similarities:

- Both are fruits.
- Both are round.
- Both can be eaten as snacks.

So, when we compare, we are looking for the similarities between things.

What does it mean to contrast?

Now, to contrast is to look at the differences. Let's go back to the example of the apple and the orange. What makes them different?

- An apple can be red or green, while an orange is, well, orange!
- An apple has a smooth skin, while the orange's skin is rougher.
- An apple's taste is sweeter, while an orange is more acidic.

So, when we contrast, we're discovering what makes things different.

Why is comparing and contrasting important?

Comparing and contrasting helps us understand the world around us better. When we compare, we see what things have in common, and this can help us make choices. For example, if you're deciding between an apple and an orange for a snack, you can compare:

- Which one do you find easier to peel?
- Which one do you like the taste of more?

This helps you decide!

Comparing and contrasting objects

Let's practice a bit more! Think about a dog and a cat. What do they have in common?

- Both are pets.
- Both have four legs.
- Both are mammals.

Now, what makes them different?

- Dogs usually enjoy going for walks, while cats prefer staying indoors.
- Dogs bark, and cats meow.
- Dogs love chasing balls, and cats enjoy playing with strings.

See how fun it is to find similarities and differences?

Using comparisons to solve problems

Comparing and contrasting can also help you solve problems. Imagine you have two pencils in front of you. One is sharpened, and the other isn't. Which one would you use to write? Probably the sharpened one, right? By comparing the two, you noticed the difference and made the right choice to solve the problem of writing.

Or imagine you have two paths to get to school: one is shorter but full of potholes, and the other is longer but smooth. By comparing them, you can choose the one that's best for you. That's the power of comparing and contrasting!

Let's practice!

Now it's your turn! How about picking two toys or two different objects and comparing them? See what they have in common and what's different. You can even do this with concepts, like comparing two sports or two types of food.

Conclusion

Now that you know how to compare and contrast, you can use this skill in many everyday situations. Whether it's deciding what to eat, which path to take, or which toy to play with, comparing and contrasting helps you make good decisions and solve problems. Always remember to look at both the similarities and the differences!

Why not start practicing now?

SIMILARITIES
DIFFERENCES
ORANGE

6-Cause and Effect

Hello, everyone! Today we are going to learn about something super important called *cause and effect*. This is the name we give when something happens because of something else. Let's understand better how it works in our daily lives!

What is cause and effect?

The *cause* is the reason why something happens. The *effect* is what happens afterward. For example, think about when you kick a ball. What happens? The ball moves, right? Kicking the ball is the cause, and the ball moving is the effect.

Let's see more examples to make it easier to understand.

Examples of cause and effect in everyday life

1. Forgetting to do your homework (*cause*) -> Getting scolded by the teacher (*effect*).
2. Watering plants every day (*cause*) -> They grow strong and green (*effect*).

3. Playing in the mud with white shoes (*cause*) -> The shoes get dirty (*effect*).

As you can see, there's always something that happens first (*the cause*) and something that happens afterward (*the effect*).

Exploring everyday scenarios

Now let's explore some situations that happen in our daily lives and see how cause and effect appear in them.

Scenario 1: Spilling a glass of juice

Imagine you're drinking juice and accidentally knock over the glass. The cause here is that the glass was pushed. And what's the effect? The juice spills on the table and makes a mess! This shows how one action (knocking over the glass) can have a consequence (spilled juice).

Scenario 2: Not going to bed early

Now imagine you went to bed late and didn't get enough rest. What happens the next day? You'll feel tired at school. The cause is going to bed late, and the effect is feeling tired.

Scenario 3: Eating too many sweets

And what if you eat too many sweets? The cause here is eating too many candies. The effect might be that you get a stomachache. So, whenever we do something, we need to think about the consequences!

How does understanding cause and effect help us?

Understanding cause and effect helps us make good decisions. If you know that something bad can happen because of an action, maybe it's better not to do it. For example, if you know that running indoors might make you fall and get hurt, you'll think twice before running, right?

It also helps us solve problems! Imagine you're playing a game, and something goes wrong. You can think: "What did I do that caused this mistake?" That way, you can change what you did to fix the problem.

Let's practice!

Now it's your turn! Think about something that happened today and ask yourself: "What was the cause of this? And what was the effect?" This will help you better understand how the world works and how the things we do have consequences.

Conclusion

Cause and effect are everywhere! From the moment you wake up until you go to bed, everything you do can have a consequence. That's why it's always good to pay attention to your actions and think about what might happen next. Remember: every cause has an effect!

How about starting now? Think about an action and what happened because of it!

7- Solving Simple Problems

Hi, everyone! Today we're going to talk about something really cool: how to solve simple problems using logical thinking. Have you ever tried to solve a puzzle or find a solution to something and wondered, "How can I figure this out?" Let's see how we can use our minds to tackle these challenges!

What is a logical problem?

A logical problem is a situation where we need to think to find the solution. Often, it's not something difficult, but we need to pay attention and use our reasoning. It's like playing with a puzzle: you keep putting pieces together until everything makes sense.

Examples of simple problems

Let's look at some examples to help you understand better:

1. **The Colored Hats Puzzle:** Imagine you have 3 hats—a red one, a blue one, and a green one. Now

you want to pick a hat to wear. If you start with the blue hat, how many hats are left to choose from? The answer is 2, because you still have the red and green hats! Easy, right?

2. **Counting Apples:** If you have 5 apples and give 2 to your friend, how many apples do you have left? You're left with 3 because 5 minus 2 equals 3. This is an example of how we use math to solve everyday problems.

3. **Organizing Toys:** You have 4 toys: a ball, a car, a doll, and a book. Which one is the largest? By thinking about the size of each item, you can say the ball is the largest toy.

How to solve these problems?

Here are some tips to help you solve simple problems:

1. **Think calmly:** Before answering, stop and think about what the problem is asking. Sometimes, just by reading carefully, you'll find the answer.

2. **Break it into parts:** If the problem seems complicated, try breaking it into smaller parts. This makes it easier to find the solution.

3. **Use examples:** Imagine the problem happening with things from your daily life. Like in the apple example, it's easier to think about a situation you know.

4. **Try different ways:** If you don't find the answer right away, think of other ways to solve it. Don't be afraid to try!

Practicing logical thinking

Let's do an exercise together!

Problem 1: João has 6 balls, and Maria has 4 balls. How many balls do they have together? The answer is 10 because 6 plus 4 equals 10. See how simple that was?

Problem 2: Ana has a blue notebook and a red one. She lends the blue notebook to Pedro. Which notebook does she still have? The red one, because the blue one is with Pedro!

These are examples of how you can use logical thinking to solve everyday challenges!

Conclusion

Solving simple problems is an important life skill! By using logic and thinking calmly, you can find solutions to challenges. Now, how about trying to create your own problems to solve? Use your imagination and have fun figuring out the answers!

8- Actions and Reactions: Conditionals

Hi, everyone! Today, we're going to talk about a very interesting idea called conditionals, or as we like to say, "if... then..." It's a way of thinking that helps us understand how things work in our daily lives. Let's explore this together!

What is "if... then..."?
The expression "if... then..." is used to explain what happens when we make a choice or a decision. It's like a rule that says: If you do one thing, then another thing will happen.

For example:

- If you throw a ball at the wall, then it will bounce back to you.
- If you study for the test, then you might get a good grade.

See? The *if* shows what you do, and the *then* shows what happens because of it.

How does this work in our lives?
The concept of "if... then..." appears all the time! Let's look at more examples to understand it better:

- If you plant a seed, then a little plant will grow.
- If you take care of your dog, then it will be happy and healthy.
- If you forget to wear a coat, then you might feel cold.

These situations show how our choices and actions affect what happens next.

Decisions and Choices

Every day, we make choices, and these choices can lead to different results. Thinking in terms of "if... then..." can help you make better decisions. Let's look at some examples:

- If I play with all my toys, then I need to put them away afterward.
- If I drink water, then I will feel more refreshed.
- If I apologize to my friend, then we can play together again.

Thinking this way helps us understand that our actions have consequences — they lead to things that happen because of what we did.

How can you use "if... then..."?

You can use "if... then..." to solve problems and make decisions. Let's practice with some questions:

1. If you keep your room tidy, then what might happen?
2. If you help your brother with his homework, then how will he feel?
3. If you eat all the fruits in your snack, then what will happen to your energy?

By thinking about the answers, you can see how the choices we make influence what comes next.

Conclusion

Understanding "if... then..." is super important because it teaches us that every action we take has a reaction. The more we think before making a decision, the better we can predict what will happen. So, how about using "if... then..." to solve problems and make smart choices every day?

If you learn this well, then you'll be ready to make great decisions in the future!

9-Organization and Planning

Hi, everyone! Today we're going to learn about something super important that can help us in many situations: organization and planning! When we know how to organize the steps to accomplish something, everything becomes easier and faster. Let's dive in with some fun examples!

How to organize steps to solve a problem?

When we have a problem to solve, it might seem complicated at first. But if we break it into smaller steps, it gets much simpler! Let's imagine you want to assemble a new toy. You need to follow the instructions in order, right? That's organization!

Here are some tips to organize the steps and solve any problem:

1. **Understand what needs to be done** – What problem do you want to solve?
2. **Break it into smaller parts** – What can you do first? Then what? What will be the last step?

3. **Follow the steps in the right order** – Go step by step until you finish what needs to be done.

For example, if your problem is tidying up your room, you can:

- First, put the toys away.
- Then, place the books on the shelf.
- Finally, make the bed.

Exercises with a sequence of actions

Now let's think about some everyday activities that require organization. Let's practice sequencing actions! Here are some examples you can try at home:

Example 1: The order of getting dressed

When you get dressed, there's an order to putting on each piece of clothing. Imagine the sequence:

1. First, put on your socks.
2. Next, put on your shirt.
3. Then, put on your pants.
4. Finally, put on your shoes.

Following this order helps you get dressed quickly without forgetting anything!

Example 2: Preparing a simple recipe

How about making a sandwich? For that, you also need a sequence of actions:

1. First, grab two slices of bread.
2. Next, spread the filling (like cheese or ham).
3. Then, add extra ingredients, like tomato or lettuce.
4. Finally, close the sandwich with the other slice of bread.

If you follow the steps in the correct order, you'll end up with a delicious sandwich ready to eat!

Planning makes a difference

Planning is when you think about what you're going to do before starting. It prevents confusion and helps save time. When you organize your ideas and make a plan, it's much easier to reach your goal. Here are some ideas to help you plan better:

- **Make a list of steps** – Write down or think about what needs to be done, like a "plan of action."
- **Be patient** – Not everything happens all at once. Follow your plan and do one thing at a time.
- **Review what you've done** – After completing each step, check if everything is okay before moving to the next one.

Conclusion

Learning to organize and plan is a very useful skill! When you know where to start and how to move forward, everything becomes easier and more fun. So, how about practicing this in your daily life? Remember: organization and planning are like a map that shows us the right way to go!

10-Deductive Reasoning

Hi, everyone! Today we're going to talk about a super interesting skill: deductive reasoning! This is a way of thinking that helps us discover new things using information we already know. It might sound complicated, but you'll see it's actually pretty cool and can be useful in many everyday situations!

What is deductive reasoning?

Deductive reasoning is when you use clues or information to come to a conclusion. It's like being a detective! Imagine you have some clues and need to figure out what they mean. Deductive reasoning helps you put these clues together and understand what's happening.

Let's look at an example:

- Clue 1: It's raining outside.
- Clue 2: When it rains, the streets get wet.

Conclusion: The street is wet because it's raining!

How does deductive reasoning work?

Deductive reasoning works like this:

1. You observe the information you have.
2. You think about the rules or facts you already know.
3. You use that information to reach an answer.

Imagine another example:

- Clue 1: All dogs like to play.
- Clue 2: Max is a dog.

Conclusion: Max likes to play.

Simple, right? With deductive reasoning, you use the information you already know to understand new things.

Concluding something from a set of information

When you have several clues, you can use them to draw conclusions. Let's do an exercise together to see how this works:

Example:

- Clue 1: Lucia is taller than Pedro.
- Clue 2: Pedro is taller than Maria.

Question: Who is taller, Lucia or Maria?

Conclusion: Lucia is taller than Maria, because Lucia is taller than Pedro and Pedro is taller than Maria!

See how we figured out something new using deductive reasoning? It's just about thinking calmly and putting the clues together!

Why is deductive reasoning important?

Deductive reasoning is really useful for solving problems and understanding the world around us. When you learn to think this way, you can:

- Solve mysteries and puzzles.
- Make safer decisions.
- Use information to understand new things.

Exercise to practice

Let's try another exercise in deductive reasoning!

- Clue 1: All cats like to sleep in the sun.
- Clue 2: Mimi is a cat.

Question: Does Mimi like to sleep in the sun?

Conclusion: Yes, Mimi likes to sleep in the sun because all cats do, and she is a cat!

Conclusion

Deductive reasoning is a powerful tool that helps us understand the world and solve problems logically. So, the next time you have some clues, remember to use deductive reasoning to figure out the answer!

11-Inductive Reasoning

Hi, everyone! Today we're going to learn about inductive reasoning, a really cool way of thinking and discovering new things. It's different from deductive reasoning, which we learned about earlier. With inductive reasoning, you observe things around you, recognize patterns, and from that, you can make predictions or imagine what might happen. Let's learn more about how this works!

What is inductive reasoning?

Inductive reasoning is like a "superpower" for noticing patterns and understanding how things repeat. When you use inductive reasoning, you observe several similar situations and, from them, create a general rule to guess what will happen next. This way of thinking helps you make predictions based on what you've already seen!

Example: Imagine that you notice that every morning, the sun rises, and the sky gets light. With this observation, you can predict that tomorrow morning, the sun will rise again and the sky will get light!

How to recognize patterns?

Patterns are sequences or repetitions we see in things around us. To recognize a pattern, observe what repeats and try to see if you can find a "rule." Let's look at an easy example:

-Example: Imagine a sequence of shapes: circle, square, circle, square, circle. What shape comes next? If you thought "square," you're right! That's because you noticed the alternating pattern between circle and square.

Recognizing patterns is very useful because it helps you understand what might happen next and predict situations.

Practical observation exercises

Let's do some exercises to practice inductive reasoning and recognize patterns. Look at the examples below and try to figure out what will come next:

1. Number sequence: 2, 4, 6, 8, ___. What number comes next?
    Answer: The number 10! The sequence follows a pattern of adding 2 to the previous number.
2. Days of the week: If today is Monday, and yesterday was Sunday, what will tomorrow be?
    Answer: Tuesday! Here, you used inductive reasoning to follow the order of the days of the week.
3. Weather prediction: If it rained every afternoon for the past three days, what's your prediction for this afternoon?
    Answer: Probably, you would say it might rain again, as you noticed the pattern from the previous days.

How to use inductive reasoning to understand the world

Inductive reasoning helps you make predictions and understand what's happening around you. By noticing patterns and repetitions, you can create a "general rule" about how things work. Of course, this rule won't always be 100% accurate, but it can give you a good idea.

Example from the animal world: If you observe several birds and notice that all of them have beaks and feathers, you can conclude that probably all birds have beaks and feathers. This is a prediction based on the observations you made!

Conclusion

Inductive reasoning is very useful for predicting what might happen and for discovering how the world works. By observing and recognizing patterns, you can make assumptions and create rules that help you better understand things. So, next time you see something repeating, think like an inductive detective and see if you can find the pattern!

12- Multi-Step Problems

Hello, everyone! Today, we're going to talk about how to solve problems that have multiple steps. Sometimes, we need to think about more than one thing to find an answer. This might seem difficult at first, but with a few tips, it gets easier. Let's learn together!

What Are Multi-Step Problems?

Some problems can't be solved with just one quick answer. Imagine you want to make a cake. You can't just mix everything together and throw it in the oven. First, you need to separate the ingredients, mix them in the right order, and only then put it in the oven. This is an example of a multi-step problem!

How to Solve Step by Step

To solve multi-step problems, we need to break the problem down into smaller parts. Let's see how to do this:

1. Read the Problem Carefully: Understand everything the problem asks for. If needed, read it again!
2. Break it Down into Smaller Parts: Take the big problem and divide it into small steps. For example, if it's a math problem, solve one calculation at a time.
3. Follow the Steps Calmly: Solve each step one at a time, without skipping any.

4. Combine All the Answers at the End: When you solve each part, put all the answers together to get the complete solution to the problem.

A Practical Example

Imagine you want to put together a big puzzle. First, you could separate the pieces by color. Then, start by assembling the edges. Slowly, you'll put the pieces in the right place until the picture is complete.

Practice at Home

Now that you know what multi-step problems are, how about practicing? Ask an adult for help to find a task with several steps, like assembling a new toy or organizing your school supplies.

Done! Now you know how to solve multi-step problems. Believe it: with practice, you'll get really good at it!

13-Puzzles and Logical Games

Hi, everyone! Let's talk about puzzles and logical games! These games are not only fun but also help exercise the brain! They teach you to think calmly and solve problems in creative ways. Ready to learn more?

What Are Puzzles and Logical Games?

Puzzles and logical games are games where you need to use reasoning to find the right answer. It's not just about luck; you have to think! When you play, you learn to observe, discover patterns, and find solutions. Each game has a different challenge, and the more you play, the easier it gets to solve!

Examples of Fun Puzzles and Games

1. **Sudoku**: Have you heard of Sudoku? It's a number game where you need to fill squares with numbers from 1 to 9, but without repeating any number in each row, column, or block. It seems tough, but it's fun and great for your brain!
2. **Traditional Puzzles**: In a jigsaw puzzle, you need to fit each piece together to form a complete picture. Start with the edges and move to the middle — soon you'll see the picture coming together!
3. **Logical Board Games**: Games like Chess and Checkers are excellent for logical thinking. Every move counts, and you need to plan ahead to win. They're great for learning strategy!

4. **Pattern-Finding Games**: There are also games where you need to find patterns, like color or shape sequences. The more patterns you spot, the faster you can solve them.

Why Are Puzzles Important?

Puzzles and logical games help your brain grow stronger and smarter. They teach patience, thinking before acting, and solving problems step by step. Plus, these games are a lot of fun!

Ready to Play?

Now that you know a bit about puzzles and logical games, why not give them a try? You can ask an adult for help learning new games or even play together! It's a great way to have fun and learn at the same time.

Have fun playing and learning!

14-Introduction to Logical Mathematics

Hi, everyone! Today we're going to learn something super interesting: how mathematics can help us solve problems logically! This means that, in addition to using numbers and doing calculations, we'll learn how to organize the steps to find an answer. We'll discover what "instructions" and "algorithms" are and see how to use them to solve problems!

Using Numbers and Simple Operations

Logical mathematics is when we use numbers, like 1, 2, 3, and also simple operations, like addition (+) and subtraction (−), to solve problems. Imagine you have 3 candies and get 2 more. To find out how many candies you have in total, you can add 3 + 2. This type of calculation helps solve small everyday challenges.

But logical mathematics is also great for solving bigger problems. Imagine you have 10 stickers and want to divide them equally between you and a friend. How do you do that? We can use a simple division to figure it out!

Instructions and Algorithms

So, what are instructions and algorithms?

- Instructions are steps you need to follow to do something. For example, when you want to make orange juice, first you need to get the orange, then squeeze it, and finally pour the juice into a glass. These steps are instructions!

- An algorithm is a sequence of instructions that leads to a result. It's like a "recipe" for solving a problem! For example, if you want to know how many candies you'll have after getting more, you can follow an algorithm that says, "1) Count how many candies you have now; 2) Add the new candies."

Exploring with Algorithms

Want to try creating an algorithm? Let's think about how to leave the house to go to the park. First, we put on our clothes, then our shoes, grab the keys, and go out the door. This is an example of an algorithm!

In mathematics, these steps help us solve problems in an organized way. When we have a challenge that seems hard, we break it down into small steps, following them one by one, until we find the solution.

Playing with Logical Mathematics

You can use what you've learned about instructions and algorithms to solve math challenges, like guessing how many coins are in a box or solving number puzzles. This makes math more fun and challenging!

Conclusion

Logical mathematics teaches us to think in an organized way and solve problems with clear steps. With numbers, simple operations, and algorithms, you can solve many challenges, like dividing, adding, or even assembling a toy by following instructions. Now that you know a bit about logical mathematics, try using these ideas in your everyday life. Have fun exploring the world of numbers and logic!

15-Conclusion and Application of Logical Thinking

Hi, everyone! Throughout our learning, we've discovered many ways to use logical thinking to solve problems and understand the world around us. Now, let's review what we've learned and see how we can use this smart thinking every day, whether at school, at home, or while playing!

Review of Learned Concepts

1. **Classification and Grouping**: We learned how to classify objects and ideas, sorting them by color, shape, size, and other characteristics. This skill helps us organize and better understand things.
2. **Sequences and Patterns**: We understood how to identify and complete patterns, like a sequence of numbers or colors. This helps us predict what comes next.
3. **Cause and Effect**: We saw that every action has a consequence. For example, if we water a plant, it grows; if we forget, it gets sad and wilts.
4. **Problem Solving**: We learned to break problems into smaller parts, solving them calmly and intelligently.
5. **Actions and Reactions**: We understood the concept of "if… then…", which helps us predict results based on the choices we make.
6. **Deductive and Inductive Reasoning**: With these types of reasoning, we learned to make conclusions based on information and recognize patterns to make predictions.

How to Use Logical Thinking in Everyday Life

At School:

- When we have math tasks, logical thinking helps us solve problems with numbers and understand sequences.
- In reading, when we analyze a story, we can use logic to predict what the character will do next.

At Home:

- Logic helps us organize our materials and toys. If we group objects by characteristics, it's easier to find them later.
- In the kitchen, we can follow a recipe step by step, thinking about what we need to do first and what comes next.

While Playing:

- In board games or puzzles, logic is important to decide the best move and solve challenges.
- When we play by building something, we use logic to choose the right pieces and make sure the structure is strong.

Why is Logical Thinking Important?

When we use logical thinking, we're able to make smarter decisions, solve problems easily, and understand the world around us better. It helps in everything, from organizing our materials to creating strategies for games and play. And the best part is that with practice, it only gets better!

So, whenever you need to solve a problem or make a decision, remember everything you've learned here. Logical thinking will be by your side, helping you find the best solutions!

Here is a series of exercises aimed at children, covering each of the 15 chapters:

1. **Introduction to Logical Thinking**

   - Question: What does it mean to think logically? Can you give an example of what logical thinking would look like?
   - Activity: On a piece of paper, draw or write a situation where it's important to think logically, like when assembling a puzzle.

2. **Basic Concepts of Logic**

   - Exercise: Mark with a "T" for true and "F" for false:
     - The sky is blue. (__)
     - An elephant is smaller than an ant. (__)
   - Challenge: Create two sentences, one true and one false, and ask someone to guess which is which.

3. **Sequences and Patterns**

   - Activity: Complete the number sequence: 2, 4, 6, __, __, 12.
   - Visual Challenge: Create a pattern using geometric shapes (e.g., circle, square, triangle) and ask a friend to guess what shape comes next.

4. **Classification and Grouping**

- Exercise: Separate the items below into two groups: fruits and animals.
    - Banana, dog, apple, cat, grape
- Activity: Take a box of colored pencils and group them by color, then group them by size.

5. Comparison and Contrast

- Question: What are the differences between a lion and a cat?
- Activity: Choose two toys or objects and describe what they have in common and what is different about them.

6. Cause and Effect

- Exercise: Think about what happens "if" you leave a ball rolling down a hill. What happens "then"?
- Activity: On a piece of paper, draw a situation that shows an event and its cause, like a glass falling and spilling water.

7. Solving Simple Problems

- Problem: If you have 3 apples and get 2 more, how many apples do you have now?
- Challenge: On your way to school, notice something that seems like a simple problem and think of a solution, like helping someone who lost a pencil.

8. Actions and Reactions: Conditionals

- Exercise: Complete the sentence: "If it's raining, then I will ____."
- Activity: Draw a situation where "if" you choose one path, "then" it leads to a specific outcome (e.g., if you

eat your snack now, then there won't be any left for later).

9. Organization and Planning

- Activity: Write or draw the steps to prepare for school (e.g., wake up, brush teeth, get dressed).
- Challenge: Make a list of actions needed to make a sandwich and organize them in the correct order.

10. Deductive Reasoning

- Exercise: If all cats have whiskers, and Toto is a cat, does he have whiskers? (__Yes / __No)
- Activity: Think of three clues for someone to guess the animal you're thinking of (e.g., lives in water, is big, has sharp teeth — answer: shark).

11. Inductive Reasoning

- Exercise: Look at the sequence and say what comes next: Sun, Moon, Sun, Moon, __.
- Activity: Look at nature (e.g., seasons) and try to identify a pattern, like leaves falling in the fall.

12. Multi-Step Problems

- Problem: You need to make a shopping list for a picnic. What do you need for that? (1. Food; 2. Drinks; 3. Games)
- Challenge: Choose a task, like assembling a toy or making a simple recipe, and break down the necessary steps to complete it.

13. Puzzles and Logical Games

- Exercise: Try to solve a 3x3 piece puzzle. How long does it take you?
- Activity: Learn the rules of a simple logic game, like Sudoku, and fill in a 4x4 grid.

14. Introduction to Mathematical Logic

- Exercise: Solve: 5 + 3 = __. Now use that answer to solve 8 - 2 = __.
- Activity: Imagine a simple algorithm for preparing for school. Write or draw each step until you leave the house.

15. Conclusion and Application of Logical Thinking

- Activity: Review one of the reasoning exercises you liked most and show someone what you learned.
- Challenge: During the next game or playtime, try to apply logical thinking. For example, if you're playing a board game, plan your next move in advance.

17-Six Thinking Hats

Here is an interactive exercise to teach Edward de Bono's "Six Thinking Hats" technique:

Objective: Use the "Six Thinking Hats" to solve a problem in a fun and creative way.

Materials:

- Six colored paper hats (or pieces of paper in the colors of the hats):
    - White (information), Red (emotions), Black (criticism), Yellow (positivity), Green (creativity), and Blue (organization).
- Pencils and paper.

Problem to Solve: "The school wants to create a new play area and needs ideas. What could be done?"

Steps:

1. **White Hat (Information):**
    - Question: "What do we already know about the available space? Is it big? Is it outdoors?"
    - Activity: List all the known facts about the space and what already exists in the school.
2. **Red Hat (Emotions):**
    - Question: "How do we feel about creating a new space? Are we excited? Is there something that worries us?"

- o Activity: Draw a happy or sad face next to the feelings and ideas about the play area.
3. **Black Hat (Caution):**
   - o Question: "Are there any problems or difficulties that might arise? What could go wrong?"
   - o Activity: List two or three things that could be a challenge (e.g., "It could rain," "There might not be enough space").
4. **Yellow Hat (Positivity):**
   - o Question: "What are the benefits and good things about this new space? How could it help the students?"
   - o Activity: Draw or write positive ideas, such as "Children can play outdoors," "It will be a fun place to make new friends."
5. **Green Hat (Creativity):**
   - o Question: "What new ideas do we have for this space? Can we think of something different, like a garden or a climbing wall?"
   - o Activity: Draw or write creative ideas that others might not have thought of.
6. **Blue Hat (Organization):**
   - o Question: "How can we organize our ideas to make everything work well? What is the next step?"
   - o Activity: Organize the ideas into a final list of what the play area should include and the steps necessary to turn the idea into reality.

Conclusion: After each hat has been used, the students review the ideas and choose the best ones to create the new play area!

About the Author

 Decio Martins de Medeiros, an electronic engineer graduated from ITA, has published books on poetry, theology, religion, management, sales, genealogy, memoirs, creativity, and entertainment.
He contributes to the *Prazer Compartilhar* blog and is a member of the *Clube de Autores*.
Check out the covers and synopses of other books by the author at:
https://www.instagram.com/authordeciomedeiros/

Logic for Children